Manganese

Richard Beatty

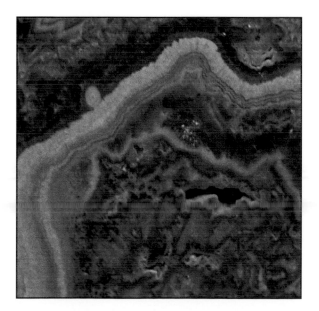

BENCHMARK BOOKS

MARSHALL CAVENDISH

NEW YORK

Benchmark Books
Marshall Cavendish
99 White Plains Road
Tarrytown, New York 10591

www.marshallcavendish.com

Library of Congress Cataloging-in-Publication Data

Beatty, Richard.
Manganese / Richard Beatty.
p.   cm. — (The elements)
Includes index.

ISBN 0-7614-1813-X
1. Manganese—Juvenile literature. I. Title. II.
Elements (Benchmark Books)
QD181.M6B43 2005
546'.541—dc22

2004047634

Printed in China

Picture credits

Front cover: 2004 RGB Research Ltd: www.element-collection.com
Back cover: NASA

2004 RGB Research Ltd: www.element-collection.com 4
Corbis: Craig Aurness 30, Lester V. Bergman 9, Paolo Fridman 12, Robert Garvey 6,
Maurice Nimmo/FLPA 1, 10, David H. Seawell 15, Penny Tweedie 13
NASA: 25
NOAA: 3, 11
Photos.com: 22/23, 26
Science & Society Picture Library: Science Museum 17, 21, 23
Science Photo Library: Andrew Lambert Photography 18, Charles D. Winters 16
Topham Picturepoint: The British Museum 7
University of Pennsylvania Library: Edgar Fahs Smith Collection 8
USDA/NRCS: Jeff Vanuga 27

Series created by The Brown Reference Group plc.
Designed by Sarah Williams
www.brownreference.com

Contents

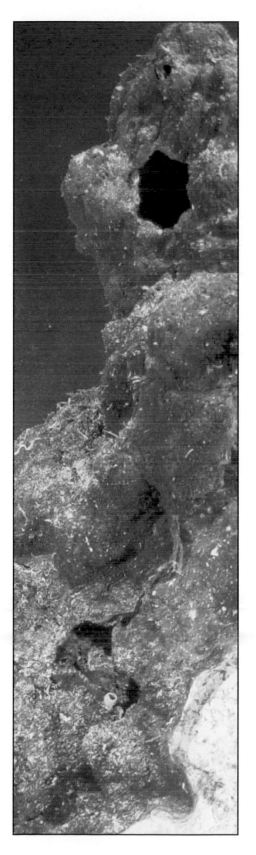

What is manganese?

Pure manganese is stored in an ampule of glass. There is a vacuum inside the ampule. This stops the manganese from reacting with oxygen in the air and keeps the metal looking shiny.

Manganese is a hard, brittle metallic element that is listed before iron in the periodic table. It is a very important ingredient of many industrial processes, especially in steel production. Manganese is used to make many things, from spacecraft to batteries. Its compounds are important for purifying water and for glazing pottery and glass. More manganese is mined in the world than any other metal except iron, aluminum, and copper.

MANGANESE FACTS	
● Chemical symbol	Mn
● Atomic number	25
● Mass number	55
● Melting point	1246 °C (2275 °F)
● Boiling point	2062 °C (3744 °F)
● Relative density	7.2
A sample of manganese weighs 7.2 times as much as the same volume of water.	

The manganese atom

Like other elements, atoms of manganese consist of a small but heavy nucleus in the center. The nucleus contains 25 positively charged particles called protons. No other element has this number of protons. Because of its number of protons manganese is said to have an atomic number of 25. Lighter, negatively charged electrons circle the nucleus. The number of electrons in an atom is the same as the number of protons. The electrons are arranged in shells. Each electron shell is surrounded by another larger one that can hold more electrons.

The nucleus of an atom contains another type of particle called a neutron. Neutrons are almost the same size as protons but have no charge. In some chemical elements, atoms exist in several forms called isotopes. Each isotope has a different number of neutrons. Manganese has only one naturally occurring isotope. This contains 30 neutrons, which gives a total of 55 particles in the nucleus of each atom. As a result, manganese has an atomic mass number of 55.

Manganese as a metal

Manganese is a hard, gray metal, similar to iron. Pure manganese metal itself is not found naturally on Earth, but only in compounds, such as manganese dioxide (MnO_2). Unlike iron, pure manganese is

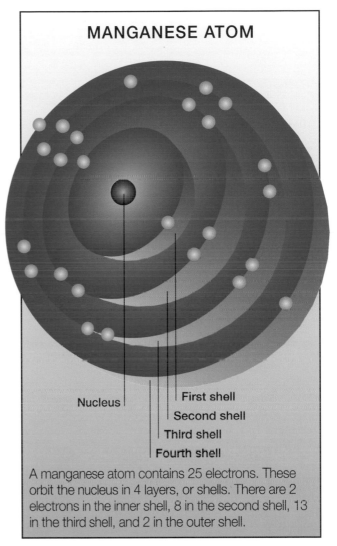

MANGANESE ATOM

Nucleus

First shell
Second shell
Third shell
Fourth shell

A manganese atom contains 25 electrons. These orbit the nucleus in 4 layers, or shells. There are 2 electrons in the inner shell, 8 in the second shell, 13 in the third shell, and 2 in the outer shell.

very brittle, and the element is only useful when mixed with other metals. Mixtures of metals are called alloys. As with most metals, a lump of manganese is made up of many microscopic crystals held tightly together. The atoms in these individual crystals pack together in different ways, depending on the temperature.

Manganese belongs to a group within the periodic table called transition metals. These elements tend to be hard, dense, and

ORIGIN OF THE NAME

The name *manganese* sounds similar to magnesium, another metallic element. Although the two elements are completely different, both names probably derive from the ancient region of Magnesia in present-day Turkey. This is where many metal ores were once mined. Long before scientists isolated the elements themselves, the names *manganese* and *magnesia* were used for various minerals that are now known to be oxides (compounds of oxygen and metals). In fact, when manganese metal was discovered, some people called it magnesium. It was only from the year 1812 onward that *magnesium* was used in its modern meaning, and the confusion was ended.

unreactive compared to other metals. Transition metals also form chemical bonds with other elements in a distinctive way. Most elements form bonds using only their outermost electron shell. Transition metals, though, can also use some of the electrons from the next shell in.

Uses of manganese

Around 90 percent of all pure manganese produced is used by the steel industry. The manganese is used mostly as an alloy ingredient but also to help get rid of impurities in the steel. Manganese metal is also often alloyed with other metals such as aluminum and copper.

Manganese compounds have a variety of important uses. Manganese dioxide, for example, is used in household batteries. In small amounts, manganese is also vital to animals and plants. Compounds such as manganese sulfate are used in fertilizers.

Manganese ore is piled high at a mine in Australia. Like most manganese ores, these rocks also contain some iron minerals.

The history of manganese

Manganese compounds were used by people long before the element itself was discovered in the late 1700s. Prehistoric peoples used manganese-containing minerals as dark pigments for their cave paintings at least 17,000 years ago. The ancient Egyptians used manganese compounds for glazing (putting shiny colored surfaces on pottery) several thousand years ago. The same compounds are still used for the same purpose even today.

Glassmakers have also used manganese minerals since early times. The Romans and others used them to remove the greenish tinge formed in glass by iron compounds. The result was a gray but see-through glass. Manganese minerals were and still are also used to color glass.

Discovery of the element

Although some elements such as sulfur, iron, and gold have been used since ancient times, it was only in the late eighteenth century that the modern idea of a chemical element began to take shape.

In particular, chemists began to suspect that many unknown elements were included in minerals they called "earths." Today we call these same substances metal oxides. In the early 1770s, Swedish chemist Carl Scheele (1742–1786) began

A pot made by Peru's Nazca culture in 200 B.C.E. is painted with black manganese oxide glaze.

7

investigating one of these earths, which he realized must contain a new element. In 1774 Scheele's friend Johan Gahn (1745–1818) first succeeded in extracting pure manganese from this compound by heating it with carbon.

Industrial developments

Once manganese was discovered, people began to mix it with other metals. During the 1850s, the first large-scale method of making steel cheaply from iron was developed by British industrialist Henry Bessemer (1813–1889). At first some batches of Bessemer's steel cracked easily. This was due to the presence of impurities such as sulfur mixed in with the metal atoms. Some steel, however, did not crack. It was discovered that the strong steel contained manganese, which removed the impurities. From 1882, manganese was being added to most steel as part of the production process.

This statue of Carl Scheele is in Stockholm, Sweden. It shows Scheele conducting an experiment.

DISCOVERERS

ROBERT HADFIELD

Robert Hadfield (1858–1940) was a British metal expert who invented the important manganese-containing steel that is now called Hadfield steel. It contains about 12 percent manganese and is strong and very hard. It is used today in heavy-duty equipment, such as railroad points, crushing equipment, and prison bars.

In the 1860s French engineer Georges Leclanché (1839–1882) began to use manganese as part of his design for electric batteries. Pure manganese was not produced on a large scale until 1941, using an electrical process.

Where manganese is found

Scientists have calculated that manganese is the twelfth most common element in Earth's crust. It is also very common in meteorites falling to Earth from outer space. It is probably present in asteroids and some comets.

Manganese in rocks

About 95 percent of the rocks in Earth's crust are formed from cooled lava or other melted material. Manganese is widespread in these rocks. However, the metal is not present in very high amounts, and it is not worth digging the rock up to extract the

This rock contains pyrolusite, a soft and dark mineral that is made up of manganese dioxide. Pyrolusite is a major type of manganese ore.

manganese. The manganese in these rocks are mostly silicates. These are compounds that contain silicon and oxygen.

Over many millions of years, rocks wear away or are chemically changed. As the changes occur, the manganese in the rocks moves to other places. These deposits make the most useful ores and are dug up by mining companies.

Scientists think that much of the manganese ores mined today were formed deep under water. Hot volcanic rocks in the deep sea heated the surrounding water. Manganese in the hot rocks dissolved in the warmed water. The manganese atoms circulated in ocean currents until they reached shallow

MANGANESE-CONTAINING MINERALS

There are over 250 known manganese-containing minerals.
This table lists some of the more important ones.

Name	Chemical formula	Chemical name	Description
manganite	$Mn_2O_3 \cdot H_2O$	manganic oxide (combined with water)	Dark, sometimes with large crystals
pyrolusite	MnO_2	manganese dioxide	Black and earthy in appearance rather than a hard rock
rhodochrosite	$MnCO_3$	manganese carbonate	A pink mineral with a glasslike shine
rhodonite	$MnSiO_3$	manganese silicate	A pink, yellow, or brown mineral, often with large crystals
wad	(no chemical formula)	(not a single mineral, but a mixture of manganese oxides)	Black with a soft, damp texture

Rhodochrosite is manganese carbonate. As this polished piece shows, the mineral's pink color makes it very different from most manganese minerals.

water, which contained more oxygen. The manganese reacted with the oxygen to form solid minerals, which settled on the seabed.

In time, these deposits became hard rock. Earth's movements may have also raised the rocks up to become dry land. The largest known deposit of manganese ore on land is in the Kalahari Desert in southern Africa. Scientists estimate that this rock was laid down in shallow water about 2 billion years ago.

The dark crust that covers this volcanic vent is a manganese compound. The vent heats the water and some of the manganese dissolves in it.

Over time, water and acids from the soil above may seep down into the ore and react with the manganese. This may make even more concentrated ores.

Underwater riches

Manganese compounds are also found on the deep-sea floor itself, as nodules. These peculiar ball-shaped objects are found by the millions in some areas. They were probably created when manganese atoms that were dissolved in the seawater came out of solution. When nodules are cut open, they show a layered structure like an onion. Manganese nodules grow very slowly—only a fraction of an inch per million years. They generally grow

around a tiny chip of rock, or sometimes even a shark's tooth. The nodules also act as shelter or anchorage for microscopic organisms. Manganese nodules also contain iron and precious metals. Some corporations have tried to mine them.

DID YOU KNOW?

DEEP SEA MYSTERY

Manganese nodules should end up buried by the ocean sediment that slowly piles up around them. It is a mystery why the nodules are found only on the surface of the deep-sea floor. One suggestion is that animals, such as fish or crabs, feed regularly on the organisms that make their home on the nodules' surfaces. Perhaps the animals roll the nodules over, preventing them from getting buried.

Mining and processing

Obtaining and processing manganese is a large worldwide industry. About 20 million tons (18 million tonnes) of manganese ore are mined every year. From this, 8 million tons (7.2 million tonnes) of manganese are extracted. Manganese is extracted from ore in a furnace at very high temperatures.

World production

Only a few countries have large reserves of manganese ore that are worth mining. Some of these, including China and Mexico, produce manganese just for their own use. The countries that produce most of the world's manganese are Australia, South Africa, Gabon in West Africa, and Brazil. Most of the ore is refined into an alloy with iron before it is sold.

Manganese ore is generally mined from open-pit mines. Since the 1970s, there have been experimental attempts to dredge up manganese nodules from the ocean floor. So far these efforts have not made money. Deep-sea mining might also cause a lot of

A mine in northern Brazil digs up manganese ore from beneath the Serra Pelada region. This mine also produces palladium, platinum, and gold.

damage to ocean ecosystems. Since no individual country owns the deep ocean floor, there might also be problems with rights and profits.

Manganese smelting

Manganese is extracted from its ore by smelting. Smelting involves two chemical reactions that take place at high temperatures. Since manganese ores are mainly oxides, refining must separate oxygen atoms from the manganese atoms to give pure manganese metal.

One way to smelt manganese is by using a tall furnace called a blast furnace. This is also the method used for smelting iron. Blast furnaces are fueled by coke, a form of coal that is nearly pure carbon. Burning this coke without much air produces carbon monoxide gas (CO).

Ground-up ore is poured in at the top of the furnace, where it reacts with carbon monoxide rising up from below. The gas takes some of the oxygen from manganese ore to make carbon dioxide (CO_2). Falling further, the ore then reacts with the carbon in the coke itself, and turns into manganese metal. The heat is so great that the metal melts and can be drained off. Non-metallic impurities, called slag, float to the surface of the molten metal and are removed separately.

Today, most manganese smelting is done in electric furnaces. As in the blast furnace, manganese ore is added at the

Manganese ores are crushed into small chips before the refining process begins. This makes smelting more efficient.

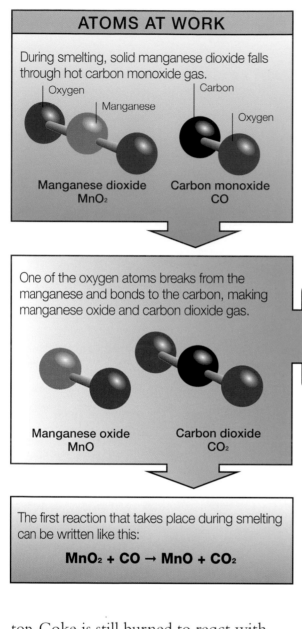

ATOMS AT WORK

During smelting, solid manganese dioxide falls through hot carbon monoxide gas.

Oxygen
Manganese
Carbon
Oxygen

Manganese dioxide
MnO_2

Carbon monoxide
CO

One of the oxygen atoms breaks from the manganese and bonds to the carbon, making manganese oxide and carbon dioxide gas.

Manganese oxide
MnO

Carbon dioxide
CO_2

The first reaction that takes place during smelting can be written like this:

$$MnO_2 + CO \rightarrow MnO + CO_2$$

so some of the final product will be iron. The main product of manganese smelting is an alloy called ferromanganese, which is manganese that also contains some iron. This is not a problem because manganese is used mainly in steelmaking, and steel is mostly made of iron.

Other metals

Manganese from the smelter is also alloyed with varying amounts of carbon and silicon. Extra processes can get rid

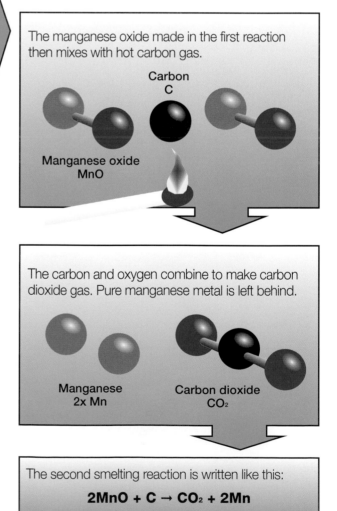

The manganese oxide made in the first reaction then mixes with hot carbon gas.

Carbon
C

Manganese oxide
MnO

The carbon and oxygen combine to make carbon dioxide gas. Pure manganese metal is left behind.

Manganese
2x Mn

Carbon dioxide
CO_2

The second smelting reaction is written like this:
$$2MnO + C \rightarrow CO_2 + 2Mn$$

top. Coke is still burned to react with the manganese ore. However, the extra energy to keep the purified metal melted into a liquid is provided by electricity, since this is generally cheaper than burning more coke.

The aim of smelting is not usually to produce pure manganese. Manganese ores always contain some iron ore as well, of most of these if needed. Smelted manganese with a lot of silicon in it is called silicomanganese. This alloy is also used to make certain steels.

Pure manganese

Pure manganese is not needed for steelmaking, and the metal is too brittle to use on its own. However, it is needed when manganese is to be alloyed with other metals, such as aluminum. Sometimes pure manganese is also used as a starting point for making manganese compounds. In one method of purifying manganese, the ore is processed and dissolved in sulfuric acid, forming manganese sulfate. Impurities such as iron, copper, and other elements, which also dissolve, are removed chemically.

Another way to purify manganese is to run a strong electric current through a pure solution of manganese sulfate. The current is run between terminals called electrodes. When manganese atoms are dissolved, they have a positive charge, so they are drawn to the negative electrode. The atoms cling to the electrode forming a thin layer of metal. Manganese made this way is almost completely pure.

A worker operates an electric furnace. Manganese is smelted using a furnace like this, which is heated by electricity as well as coke fuel. Manganese ores often contain iron, and the two metals are smelted together.

Chemistry and compounds

Compounds containing manganese have many practical uses, from purifying water to decorating pottery. Manganese's chemistry is also useful because it is so varied.

Chemical properties

Manganese belongs to the set of elements called the transition metals. This set includes other important metals such as iron and copper. The transition metals share many properties. They are mainly hard, heavy, and have high melting points. They often also form brightly colored compounds. Some of manganese's chemistry is like that of iron, its neighbor in the periodic table. Like iron, manganese slowly combines with oxygen in dry air, but rusts in moist air.

Hydrogen peroxide (H_2O_2) breaks down into water and oxygen gas when it is mixed with a manganese dioxide (MnO_2) catalyst. The catalyst is added to the liquid hydrogen peroxide as granules.

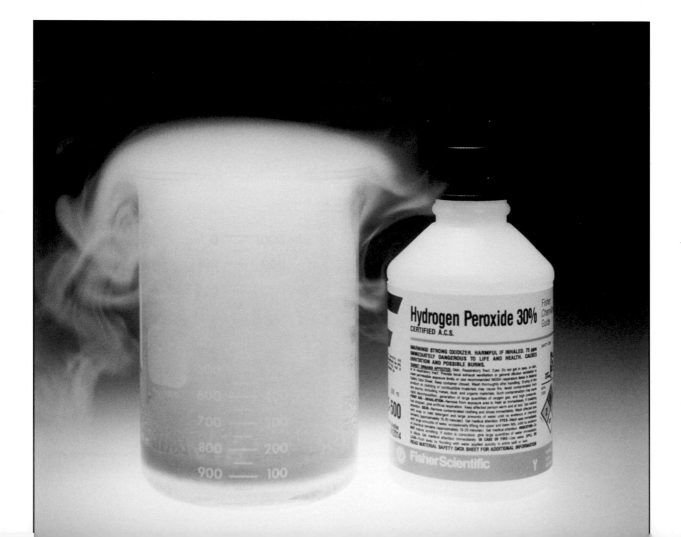

Manganese dioxide

Manganese dioxide (MnO_2), a crumbly black solid, is the most important manganese compound. As the most common manganese ore, it is the main starting point for making manganese metal and other manganese compounds.

Manganese dioxide is specially processed to be used in many ways. In chemical reactions, manganese dioxide is important in two ways. Sometimes it takes part in the reaction itself. It is also used as a catalyst. Catalysts are substances that make reactions go faster without being altered in the process. For example, manganese dioxide is used as a catalyst when making an artificial vanilla flavoring called vanillin.

A model of Georges Leclanché's battery shows the carbon rod surrounded by manganese dioxide granules. This type of battery was safer than earlier designs. It did not contain dangerous liquid acids and was known as a "dry cell."

DID YOU KNOW?

HOW BATTERIES WORK

All batteries involve two separate but linked chemical reactions going on inside them. The reactions are centered around two structures, which chemists call electrodes. Other people may describe them as electric terminals. One of the reactions releases electrons, while the other collects them. When the electrodes of a battery are connected to an electric circuit, electrons flow through the wire from one electrode to the other. This electric current keeps the chemical reactions going. The electrical energy produced by the two reactions can be used to power anything from an electric car to a watch.

Manganese dioxide is also used in electric batteries. French engineer Georges Leclanché (1839–1882) was the first to use manganese dioxide in this way. In 1866, Leclanché invented a new and inexpensive battery where one electrode (terminal) was made of zinc. The other was a mixture of powdered manganese dioxide and

Purple potassium permanganate ($KMnO_4$) crystals dissolve in water. The compound splits into two ions— potassium (K^+) and permanganate ($KMnO_4^-$).

carbon, packed around a carbon core. Modern batteries have a design that is similar to Leclanché's battery.

Potassium permanganate

Another important manganese compound is potassium permanganate ($KMnO_4$). This is a purple substance that is often used in high school laboratories to color water. In this compound, manganese is combined with four oxygen atoms to form a negatively charged ion (MnO_4^-). This is attracted to the positive potassium ion (K^+) and the two bond together.

Potassium permanganate forms black crystals that dissolve in water to give a deep purple solution. It is a very important purifying agent and reacts with a wide variety of harmful substances to make them harmless. Potassium permanganate is widely used in purifying drinking water and treating wastewater and toxic waste. It is also used in the laboratory to show if something is an acid or base.

MANGANESE IN POTTERY

Manganese compounds have been used to color clay and glass for thousands of years. They are still used as important coloring agents in pottery. The colored compounds may be added to the clay before it is molded into the correct shape. Otherwise the manganese is used as part of the decorative glaze that is spread over the surface of finished pots. Manganese dioxide (MnO_2) and manganese carbonate ($MnCO_3$) are both used. The colors produced can range from dark brown to pink and violet. Clay pots are hardened in an oven called a kiln. The potter controls the color of the glaze by varying the temperature and amount of air in the kiln as the pot is hardened. The color is also affected by the acidity of the glaze and whether other chemicals are also used.

Other manganese compounds

Manganese forms many simple compounds, such as manganese sulfate ($MnSO_4$) and manganese nitrate ($MnNO_3$). These two compounds dissolve in water. This means that manganese can be absorbed by plant roots. Plants need this manganese to grow, but some soils do not have enough. Manganese sulfate and nitrate are added to fertilizers to help plants grow.

Oxidation numbers

Atoms form bonds with each other using their outer electrons. Some bonds form because an atom transfers an electron to

ATOMS AT WORK

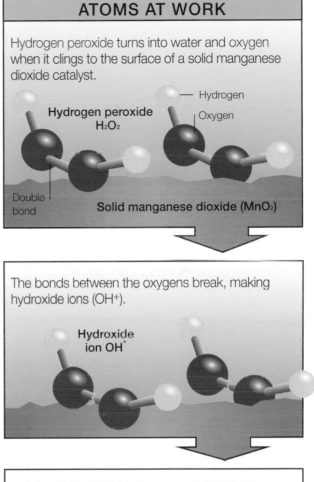

Hydrogen peroxide turns into water and oxygen when it clings to the surface of a solid manganese dioxide catalyst.

Hydrogen peroxide H_2O_2 — Hydrogen — Oxygen

Double bond

Solid manganese dioxide (MnO_2)

The bonds between the oxygens break, making hydroxide ions (OH^+).

Hydroxide ion OH^+

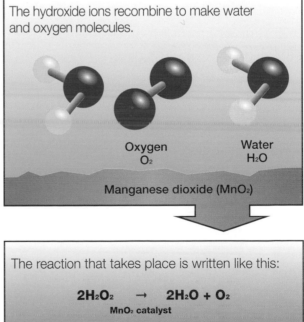

The hydroxide ions recombine to make water and oxygen molecules.

Oxygen O_2 Water H_2O

Manganese dioxide (MnO_2)

The reaction that takes place is written like this:

$$2H_2O_2 \rightarrow 2H_2O + O_2$$

MnO_2 catalyst

another atom. The two atoms are then held together because they have opposite electrical charges. An example is the Mn^{2+} ion found in manganese sulfate ($MnSO_4$). Here, the manganese atom has lost two of its electrons to the sulfate (SO_4^{2-}) part of the compound. In other manganese compounds, electrons are shared between atoms, rather than completely transferred.

Even when electrons are shared in a chemical bond, the manganese partly loses control of these electrons to the other atom involved—to an oxygen atom, for instance. Chemists use an oxidation number to show how many electrons an atom has lost control of after a reaction.

Names and numbers

In manganese dioxide (MnO_2), for example, the manganese atom has an oxidation number of $+4$. This means that it has lost control of four electrons to the two oxygen atoms. Manganese's oxidation number within a compound is often included as Roman numerals in the compound's chemical name. For example, MnO_2 can also be written manganese (IV) oxide. In fact, a lot of manganese's chemical reactions involve it switching from one oxidation number, or oxidation state, to another. Whenever a manganese atom increases its oxidation number in a reaction, it is oxidized. When it decreases its oxidation number, it is reduced.

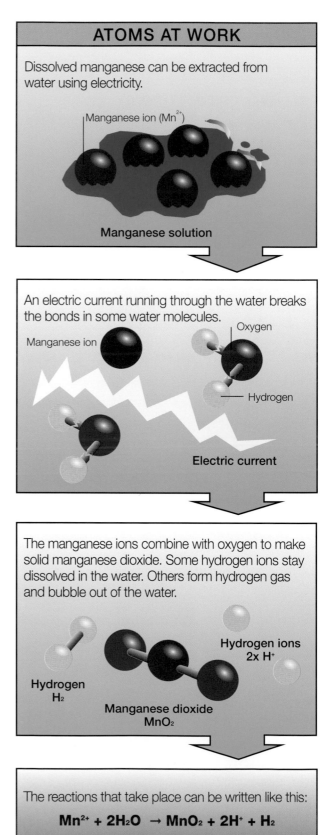

ATOMS AT WORK

Dissolved manganese can be extracted from water using electricity.

Manganese ion (Mn^{2+})

Manganese solution

An electric current running through the water breaks the bonds in some water molecules.

Manganese ion

Oxygen

Hydrogen

Electric current

The manganese ions combine with oxygen to make solid manganese dioxide. Some hydrogen ions stay dissolved in the water. Others form hydrogen gas and bubble out of the water.

Hydrogen ions
$2x\ H^+$

Hydrogen
H_2

Manganese dioxide
MnO_2

The reactions that take place can be written like this:

$$Mn^{2+} + 2H_2O \rightarrow MnO_2 + 2H^+ + H_2$$

Manganese in steel

Steel is vital to modern civilization. People use it to make everything from skyscrapers and ships to surgical instruments and paperclips. The main ingredient of steel is the element iron, but manganese is also an essential ingredient. In fact, modern steelmaking would be impossible without manganese. Around 90 percent of the manganese produced worldwide is used by the steel industry.

These cubes of manganese steel contain about 12 percent manganese. It is a very tough alloy and is not magnetic. Manganese steel was developed in 1882 by English engineer Robert Hadfield (1858–1940).

Understanding steel

Steel is iron with a small, but carefully controlled, amount of carbon mixed in with it. Some steels also have other metals that are alloyed (mixed or combined) with the iron as well. Like other metals, steel is made of many microscopic crystals bound tightly together. The atoms in these crystals are usually able to slide past each other a small amount if they are pushed or pulled. This means that the metal can bend and will not crack too easily.

Like most pure metals, pure iron is too soft to be used on its own. Adding carbon makes the metal stronger and harder.

Before manganese was used in steelmaking, steel was brittle. Early steel railroad tracks often cracked. Modern rails, like these, are made with manganese steel.

Too much carbon, however, will make the steel very hard but also very brittle and likely to shatter.

Under the microscope, steel has a complex structure. Some crystals are made of pure iron. There are others in which iron is combined with carbon. The size and type of crystals present in the steel depend on how the steel has been made. People have made steel from iron in small amounts for thousands of years, before

Bessemer took impure iron, and converted it to steel in a container by blowing air through it. The oxygen in the air burned off the extra carbon and any other impurities present.

Manganese to the rescue

Bessemer's method was far quicker and more economical than other methods, but at first it did not work properly. His steel often cracked. People later learned

its microscopic structure was understood. It was used to make swords, for example. It was not until the mid-1800s, however, that methods were invented for producing steel on a large scale. British industrialist Henry

Manganese steel is very tough. It was used to make soldier's helmets in World War I (1914–1918). This helmet has been tested for strength. The dents were caused by bullets fired at the helmet.

23

that the secret to strong steel was adding a little manganese to it. The manganese combined with some of the extra oxygen mixed in with the hot liquid metal. At the same time, manganese atoms combined with impurities, which would otherwise weaken the metal.

Manganese as an alloy

Today, virtually all steel has some manganese in it to give it added strength. With just one or two percent manganese, steel objects are made lighter but are just as strong. This makes the steel useful for making cars and other vehicles. Steel with about 12 percent manganese, sometimes called Hadfield steel, is particularly hard. Steels with an even higher manganese content have other useful properties. They are non-magnetic and are able to withstand cold conditions.

The element sulfur is a big problem in steelmaking because it combines with iron to form iron sulfide (FeS). This compound forms separate crystals when the metal cools into a solid. This weakens the steel, making it crack when heated. Manganese can solve this problem by combining with the sulfur instead, making manganese sulfide (MnS). This manganese sulfide forms small particles that do not affect the steel's strength. Some of it also separates out from the metal and can be skimmed off in the slag.

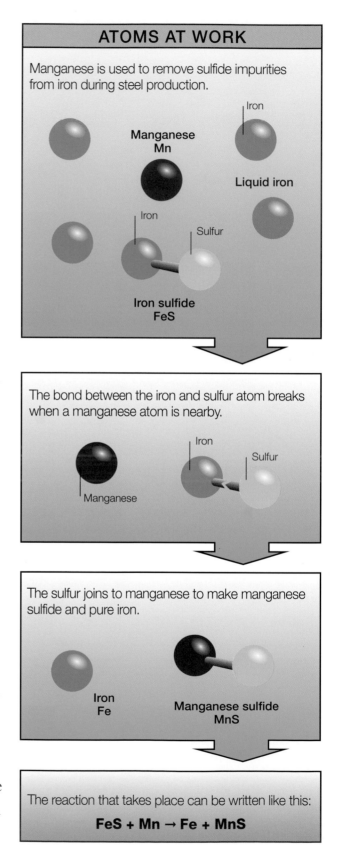

ATOMS AT WORK

Manganese is used to remove sulfide impurities from iron during steel production.

Iron

Manganese
Mn

Liquid iron

Iron

Sulfur

Iron sulfide
FeS

The bond between the iron and sulfur atom breaks when a manganese atom is nearby.

Iron

Sulfur

Manganese

The sulfur joins to manganese to make manganese sulfide and pure iron.

Iron
Fe

Manganese sulfide
MnS

The reaction that takes place can be written like this:

$$FeS + Mn \rightarrow Fe + MnS$$

Other manganese alloys

Manganese is also combined with other metals, such as aluminum and copper, to make important alloys. Only small amounts of manganese can be alloyed with aluminum before the metal becomes too brittle. Even these small percentages, though, make the aluminum stronger and more useful. The manganese protects the aluminum by combining with

impurities that would otherwise corrode aluminum. This is especially important when aluminum is used to hold food and drink in pots and pans. The largest use of manganese–aluminum alloys is for soda and beer cans. Billions of cans are produced every year.

Larger amounts of manganese can be mixed with copper than with aluminum. Just one or two percent manganese makes the copper stronger. It also makes the copper easier to cast (pour into molds) when melted. Other copper alloys with more manganese are used in temperature control devices and the non-magnetic parts of watches.

The Gemini spacecraft, such as this one from 1965, were made from manganese-aluminum alloys.

Manganese and living things

Today, scientists are making exciting new discoveries about the role of manganese in living things. Even though animals and plants need only very small amounts of manganese, it appears that the element is vital to a healthy life.

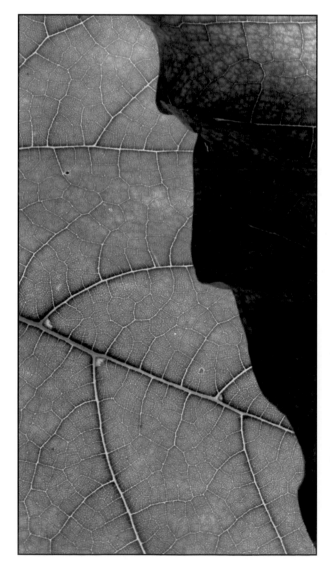

DID YOU KNOW?

LONG-TERM DANGERS

Manganese is not generally considered dangerous, especially since very small amounts are eaten naturally as part of our diet. However, people who work with powdered manganese compounds need to be careful. This is because breathing in any manganese-containing dust may damage the lungs. Some miners and metalworkers may develop a serious disease called manganism after years of exposure to manganese. This affects the nervous system and can cause symptoms similar to Parkinson's disease, including difficulty with body movements.

Keeping control

In living cells, chemical reactions are controlled by molecules called enzymes. Enzymes, which are mainly protein, are biological catalysts. An enzyme's complex shape helps it bring substances together so they react with each other.

Some important enzymes have atoms of manganese right at their center. From bacteria to humans, enzymes containing manganese protect cell membranes and other delicate structures against attack from dangerously reactive molecules. Because manganese can switch between different oxidation states, it has the power

The enzymes that trap energy in sunlight during photosynthesis in leaves contain manganese.

Some farmers add manganese to their soils to keep their crops healthy.

to react temporarily with high-energy molecules, allowing the enzyme to capture and destroy the danger.

Photosynthesis, the process by which green plants produce their own food using the Sun's energy, also requires manganese. At the end of photosynthesis, oxygen is released into the air. This final oxygen-releasing step is controlled by an enzyme that contains four manganese atoms. The manganese helps with the difficult task of handling oxygen atoms within the cell, before they are safely released as oxygen molecules (O_2).

Today, scientists are studying this enzyme very carefully. They hope that by understanding how plants produce their food, we may be able to imitate this process artificially. We could then make better use of the Sun's energy.

Getting enough

Animals and plants both need manganese to survive. The human body contains about 0.0007 ounces (20 milligrams) of manganese. We probably only need 0.0001 ounces (3 milligrams) per day to survive. Grains, nuts, and vegetables provide more manganese than meat. However, too much manganese can interfere with the way the body absorbs other minerals.

Plants may sometimes need extra manganese if there is not enough of the element in the soil. Manganese sulfate ($MnSO_4$) and manganese oxide (MnO) are the most common compounds added to fertilizers for this purpose.

Periodic table

Everything in the universe is made from combinations of substances called elements. Elements are made of tiny particles called atoms. These are far too small for people to see.

The character of an atom depends on how many even tinier particles called protons there are in its center, or nucleus. An element's atomic number is the same as its number of protons.

Scientists have found around 110 different elements. About 90 elements occur naturally on Earth. The rest have been made in experiments.

All these elements are set out on a chart called the periodic table. This lists all the elements in order according to their atomic number.

The elements at the left of the table are metals. Those at the right are nonmetals. Between the metals and the nonmetals are the metalloids, which sometimes act like metals and sometimes like nonmetals.

● On the left of the table are the alkali metals. These elements have just one electron in their outer shells.

● On the right of the periodic table are the noble gases. These elements have full outer shells.

● Elements in the same group have the same number of electrons in their outer shells.

● Elements get more reactive as you go down a group.

● The number of electrons orbiting the nucleus increases down each group.

● The transition metals are in the middle of the table, between Groups II and III.

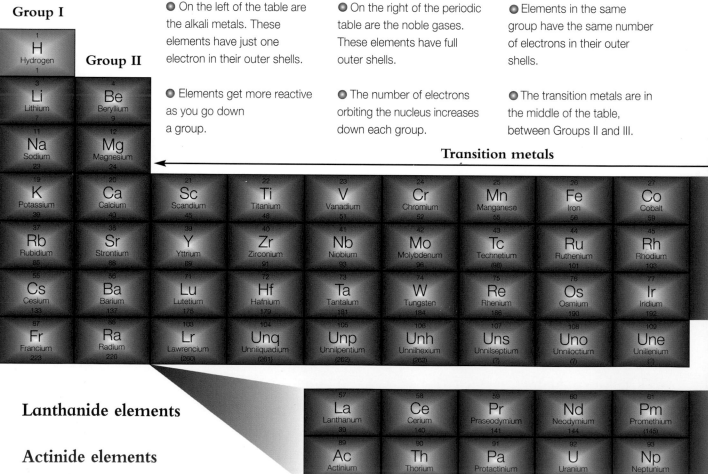

Group I

Group II

Transition metals

Lanthanide elements

Actinide elements

The horizontal rows are called periods. As you go across a period, the atomic number increases by one from each element to the next. The vertical columns are called groups. Elements get heavier as you go down a group. All the elements in a group have the same number of electrons in their outer shells. This means that they react in similar ways.

The transition metals fall between Groups II and III. Their electron shells fill up in an unusual way. The lanthanide elements and the actinide elements are set apart from the main table to make it easier to read. All the lanthanide elements and the actinide elements are quite rare.

Manganese in the table

Manganese is in the first period of the transition metals. Like other transition metals, manganese atoms have empty spaces in both their two outermost electron shells. This allows them to form complex ions, which can have a variety of charges. Manganese compounds have several colors, such as purple, black, and red.

Metals
Metalloids (semimetals)
Nonmetals

25
Mn
Manganese
55

Atomic (proton) number
Symbol
Name
Atomic mass

Group VIII

Group III	Group IV	Group V	Group VI	Group VII	
					2 He Helium 4
5 B Boron 11	6 C Carbon 12	7 N Nitrogen 14	8 O Oxygen 16	9 F Fluorine 19	10 Ne Neon 20
13 Al Aluminum 27	14 Si Silicon 28	15 P Phosphorus 31	16 S Sulfur 32	17 Cl Chlorine 35	18 Ar Argon 40

28 Ni Nickel 59	29 Cu Copper 64	30 Zn Zinc 65	31 Ga Gallium 70	32 Ge Germanium 73	33 As Arsenic 75	34 Se Selenium 79	35 Br Bromine 80	36 Kr Krypton 84
46 Pd Palladium 106	47 Ag Silver 108	48 Cd Cadmium 112	49 In Indium 115	50 Sn Tin 119	51 Sb Antimony 122	52 Te Tellurium 128	53 I Iodine 127	54 Xe Xenon 131
78 Pt Platinum 195	79 Au Gold 197	80 Hg Mercury 201	81 Tl Thallium 204	82 Pb Lead 207	83 Bi Bismuth 209	84 Po Polonium (209)	85 At Astatine (210)	86 Rn Radon (222)

62 Sm Samarium 150	63 Eu Europium 152	64 Gd Gadolinium 157	65 Tb Terbium 159	66 Dy Dysprosium 163	67 Ho Holmium 165	68 Er Erbium 167	69 Tm Thulium 169	70 Yb Ytterbium 173
94 Pu Plutonium (244)	95 Am Americium (243)	96 Cm Curium (247)	97 Bk Berkelium (247)	98 Cf Californium (251)	99 Es Einsteinium (252)	100 Fm Fermium (257)	101 Md Mendelevium (258)	102 No Nobelium (259)

Chemical reactions

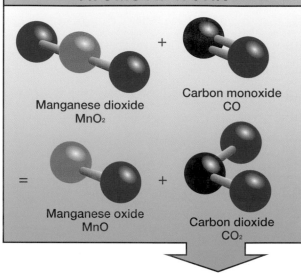

ATOMS AT WORK

Manganese dioxide
MnO₂

Carbon monoxide
CO

Manganese oxide
MnO

Carbon dioxide
CO₂

Chemical reactions are going on around us all the time. Some reactions involve just two substances, others many more. But whenever a reaction takes place, at least one substance is changed.

In a chemical reaction, the atoms stay the same. But they join up in different combinations to form new molecules.

Writing an equation

Chemical reactions can be described by writing down the atoms and molecules before and after the reactions.

The reaction that takes place when manganese dioxide reacts with carbon monoxide is written like this:

$MnO_2 + CO \rightarrow MnO + CO_2$

This tells us that one molecule of manganese dioxide reacts with one molecule of carbon monoxide to make one molecule of manganese oxide and one molecule of carbon dioxide.

The red colors in the cliffs of Cedar Breaks National Monument in Utah are caused by manganese oxides

Since the atoms stay the same, the number of atoms before will be the same as the number of atoms after. Chemists write the reaction as an equation. This shows what happens in the chemical reaction.

Making it balance

When the numbers of each atom on both sides of the equation are equal, the equation is balanced. If the numbers are not equal, something is wrong. The chemist adjusts the number of atoms involved until the equation balances.

Glossary

acidity: How much acid a substance has. An acid is a chemical that releases hydrogen ions easily during reactions.

atom: The smallest part of an element having all the properties of that element. Each atom is less than a millionth of an inch in diameter.

atomic mass number: The number of protons and neutrons in an atom.

atomic number: The number of protons in the nucleus of an atom.

bond: The attraction between two atoms, or ions, that holds them together.

compound: A new substance made when two or more elements chemically join together.

corrosion: The eating away of a material by reaction with other chemicals, often oxygen and moisture in the air.

crystal: A solid consisting of a repeating pattern of atoms, ions, or molecules.

electrode: A material that exchanges electrons with another electrode.

electron: A tiny particle with a negative charge. Electrons are found inside atoms, where they move around the nucleus in layers called electron shells.

element: A substance that is made from only one type of atom. Manganese belongs to a group of elements called the transition metals.

equation: An expression using numbers and symbols to explain how a chemical reaction takes place.

ion: An atom or a group of atoms that has lost or gained electrons to become electrically charged.

metal: An element on the left-hand side of the periodic table.

mineral: A compound or element as it is found in its natural form in Earth.

molecule: A particle that contains atoms held together by chemical bonds.

neutron: A tiny particle with no electrical charge. Neutrons are found in the nucleus of almost every atom.

nucleus: The dense structure at the center of an atom. Protons and neutrons are found inside the nucleus of an atom.

periodic table: A chart of all the chemical elements laid out in order of their atomic number.

proton: A tiny particle with a positive charge. Protons are found inside the nucleus of an atom.

reaction: A process in which two or more elements or compounds combine to produce new substances.

solution: A liquid that has another substance dissolved in it.

transition metal: An element positioned in the middle of the periodic table. Transition metals, including manganese, have spaces in their outer electron shell and in the next shell in.

Index